50 Modern Vegetarian Table Recipes

By: Kelly Johnson

Table of Contents

- Avocado Toast with Radishes & Microgreens
- Quinoa & Roasted Veggie Buddha Bowl
- Sweet Potato & Black Bean Tacos
- Chickpea & Spinach Curry
- Cauliflower Buffalo Wings
- Roasted Beet & Goat Cheese Salad
- Miso-Glazed Eggplant
- Spaghetti Squash with Pesto
- Grilled Halloumi & Watermelon Salad
- Mushroom & Truffle Risotto
- Lentil Shepherd's Pie
- Zucchini Noodles with Avocado Sauce
- Thai Peanut Tofu Stir-Fry
- Charred Brussels Sprouts with Balsamic Glaze
- Butternut Squash & Sage Ravioli
- Korean BBQ Jackfruit Tacos
- Vegan Mac & Cheese
- Portobello Mushroom Burgers
- Mediterranean Chickpea Salad
- Ratatouille with Garlic Bread
- Soba Noodles with Sesame-Ginger Dressing
- Roasted Cauliflower Steaks with Chimichurri
- Moroccan Spiced Carrot & Lentil Soup
- Spinach & Ricotta Stuffed Peppers
- Vegan Sushi Rolls with Mango & Avocado
- Black Bean & Quinoa Stuffed Sweet Potatoes
- Creamy Tomato Basil Soup with Grilled Cheese
- Thai Green Curry with Vegetables
- Spicy Kimchi Fried Rice
- Crispy Polenta with Roasted Mushrooms
- Grilled Corn & Avocado Salad
- Pumpkin & Sage Gnocchi
- Roasted Red Pepper Hummus with Pita Chips
- Mango & Coconut Chia Pudding
- Vegan Tofu Scramble Breakfast Tacos

- Balsamic Glazed Roasted Carrots
- Indian Daal with Garlic Naan
- Stuffed Acorn Squash with Cranberries & Pecans
- Cabbage & Peanut Slaw with Lime Dressing
- Vegan Lasagna with Cashew Cheese
- Mediterranean Stuffed Eggplant
- Roasted Garlic & Cauliflower Soup
- Vegan Poke Bowl with Marinated Tofu
- Kale Caesar Salad with Crispy Chickpeas
- Spiced Lentil & Sweet Potato Stew
- Warm Farro Salad with Roasted Vegetables
- Black Bean & Corn Enchiladas
- Jackfruit BBQ Sandwiches
- Japanese-Inspired Miso Glazed Tofu Bowl
- Vegan Chocolate Avocado Mousse

Avocado Toast with Radishes & Microgreens

Ingredients:

- 2 slices sourdough or whole-grain bread
- 1 ripe avocado
- ½ lemon, juiced
- Salt & pepper, to taste
- 2 radishes, thinly sliced
- Handful of microgreens
- Drizzle of olive oil

Instructions:

1. Toast the bread to your liking.
2. Mash the avocado with lemon juice, salt, and pepper.
3. Spread the avocado mixture onto toast.
4. Top with radish slices and microgreens.
5. Drizzle with olive oil and serve.

Quinoa & Roasted Veggie Buddha Bowl

Ingredients:

- 1 cup quinoa, cooked
- 1 cup roasted sweet potatoes, cubed
- 1 cup roasted chickpeas
- ½ cup cherry tomatoes, halved
- ½ avocado, sliced
- Handful of baby spinach
- Tahini dressing

Instructions:

1. Cook quinoa according to package instructions.
2. Roast sweet potatoes and chickpeas at 400°F (200°C) for 20–25 minutes.
3. Assemble the bowl with quinoa, roasted veggies, tomatoes, avocado, and spinach.
4. Drizzle with tahini dressing and serve.

Sweet Potato & Black Bean Tacos

Ingredients:

- 1 medium sweet potato, diced
- 1 cup black beans, drained & rinsed
- ½ tsp cumin
- ½ tsp smoked paprika
- Corn tortillas
- ½ avocado, sliced
- ¼ cup red onion, diced
- Fresh cilantro

Instructions:

1. Roast sweet potatoes with olive oil, cumin, and paprika at 400°F (200°C) for 20 minutes.
2. Heat black beans in a pan and season with salt.
3. Warm tortillas, then fill with sweet potatoes, black beans, avocado, and onion.
4. Garnish with cilantro and serve.

Chickpea & Spinach Curry

Ingredients:

- 1 can chickpeas, drained
- 2 cups fresh spinach
- 1 onion, diced
- 2 cloves garlic, minced
- 1 tbsp curry powder
- 1 can coconut milk
- 1 tbsp tomato paste

Instructions:

1. Sauté onion and garlic in oil until soft.
2. Add curry powder and tomato paste, cook for 1 minute.
3. Stir in chickpeas and coconut milk, simmer for 10 minutes.
4. Add spinach and cook until wilted. Serve with rice.

Cauliflower Buffalo Wings

Ingredients:

- 1 head cauliflower, cut into florets
- 1 cup flour
- 1 cup water
- 1 tsp garlic powder
- ½ tsp salt
- ½ cup hot sauce
- 2 tbsp melted butter

Instructions:

1. Preheat oven to 425°F (220°C).
2. Mix flour, water, garlic powder, and salt into a batter.
3. Dip cauliflower in the batter and place on a baking sheet.
4. Bake for 20 minutes.
5. Mix hot sauce with melted butter, coat cauliflower, and bake for another 10 minutes.

Roasted Beet & Goat Cheese Salad

Ingredients:

- 2 roasted beets, sliced
- 2 cups mixed greens
- ¼ cup goat cheese, crumbled
- ¼ cup walnuts, toasted
- 2 tbsp balsamic glaze

Instructions:

1. Toss greens with beets, goat cheese, and walnuts.
2. Drizzle with balsamic glaze and serve.

Miso-Glazed Eggplant

Ingredients:

- 1 eggplant, halved
- 2 tbsp miso paste
- 1 tbsp soy sauce
- 1 tbsp maple syrup
- 1 tbsp sesame oil

Instructions:

1. Preheat oven to 400°F (200°C).
2. Mix miso, soy sauce, maple syrup, and sesame oil.
3. Score eggplant and brush with glaze.
4. Roast for 20–25 minutes.

Spaghetti Squash with Pesto

Ingredients:

- 1 spaghetti squash
- ½ cup pesto
- ¼ cup cherry tomatoes, halved
- 2 tbsp pine nuts

Instructions:

1. Roast spaghetti squash at 400°F (200°C) for 40 minutes.
2. Scrape out the strands and mix with pesto.
3. Top with cherry tomatoes and pine nuts.

Grilled Halloumi & Watermelon Salad

Ingredients:

- ½ block halloumi cheese, sliced
- 2 cups watermelon, cubed
- 1 handful fresh mint
- 1 tbsp balsamic glaze

Instructions:

1. Grill halloumi until golden on both sides.
2. Combine with watermelon and mint.
3. Drizzle with balsamic glaze and serve.

Mushroom & Truffle Risotto

Ingredients:

- 1 cup Arborio rice
- 3 cups vegetable broth
- 1 cup mushrooms, sliced
- ½ cup Parmesan cheese
- 1 tbsp truffle oil

Instructions:

1. Sauté mushrooms in oil. Add rice and toast for 2 minutes.
2. Gradually add broth, stirring constantly, until rice is creamy.
3. Stir in Parmesan and truffle oil.

Lentil Shepherd's Pie

Ingredients:

- 1 cup cooked lentils
- 1 carrot, diced
- 1 onion, diced
- 2 cloves garlic, minced
- 1 cup vegetable broth
- 2 cups mashed potatoes

Instructions:

1. Sauté onion, carrot, and garlic. Add lentils and broth, simmer for 10 minutes.
2. Spread into a baking dish and top with mashed potatoes.
3. Bake at 375°F (190°C) for 20 minutes.

Zucchini Noodles with Avocado Sauce

Ingredients:

- 2 medium zucchinis, spiralized
- 1 ripe avocado
- ½ cup fresh basil
- 1 clove garlic
- 1 tbsp lemon juice
- 2 tbsp olive oil
- Salt & pepper to taste

Instructions:

1. Blend avocado, basil, garlic, lemon juice, olive oil, salt, and pepper until smooth.
2. Toss with spiralized zucchini noodles and serve.

Thai Peanut Tofu Stir-Fry

Ingredients:

- 1 block firm tofu, cubed
- 1 red bell pepper, sliced
- 1 cup broccoli florets
- ½ cup snow peas
- ¼ cup peanut butter
- 2 tbsp soy sauce
- 1 tbsp maple syrup
- 1 tsp sesame oil

Instructions:

1. Pan-fry tofu until golden brown, then set aside.
2. Stir-fry bell pepper, broccoli, and snow peas for 5 minutes.
3. Mix peanut butter, soy sauce, maple syrup, and sesame oil.
4. Add tofu and sauce to the pan, toss, and serve.

Charred Brussels Sprouts with Balsamic Glaze

Ingredients:

- 2 cups Brussels sprouts, halved
- 2 tbsp olive oil
- 2 tbsp balsamic glaze
- Salt & pepper

Instructions:

1. Sear Brussels sprouts in a hot pan with olive oil until charred.
2. Drizzle with balsamic glaze and season with salt and pepper.

Butternut Squash & Sage Ravioli

Ingredients:

- 1 cup mashed roasted butternut squash
- ½ tsp dried sage
- 1 tbsp nutritional yeast
- 1 package vegan wonton wrappers

Instructions:

1. Mix squash, sage, and nutritional yeast.
2. Fill wonton wrappers with the mixture, seal edges.
3. Boil for 3 minutes, then serve with your favorite sauce.

Korean BBQ Jackfruit Tacos

Ingredients:

- 1 can young jackfruit, shredded
- 2 tbsp Korean BBQ sauce
- ½ cup shredded cabbage
- 4 small tortillas

Instructions:

1. Sauté jackfruit in a pan with BBQ sauce for 10 minutes.
2. Serve in tortillas with shredded cabbage.

Vegan Mac & Cheese

Ingredients:

- 2 cups elbow pasta
- 1 cup soaked cashews
- ½ cup nutritional yeast
- 1 cup plant-based milk
- 1 tsp garlic powder
- 1 tsp Dijon mustard

Instructions:

1. Cook pasta according to package directions.
2. Blend cashews, nutritional yeast, milk, garlic powder, and mustard until creamy.
3. Mix with pasta and serve.

Portobello Mushroom Burgers

Ingredients:

- 2 large portobello mushrooms
- 2 tbsp balsamic vinegar
- 1 tbsp olive oil
- ½ tsp garlic powder
- Burger buns & toppings

Instructions:

1. Marinate mushrooms in balsamic vinegar, olive oil, and garlic powder.
2. Grill for 5 minutes per side.
3. Serve in buns with toppings.

Mediterranean Chickpea Salad

Ingredients:

- 1 can chickpeas, drained
- ½ cup cherry tomatoes, halved
- ¼ cup red onion, diced
- ¼ cup cucumber, diced
- 1 tbsp olive oil
- 1 tbsp lemon juice

Instructions:

1. Mix all ingredients in a bowl and serve chilled.

Ratatouille with Garlic Bread

Ingredients:

- 1 zucchini, sliced
- 1 eggplant, sliced
- 1 red bell pepper, diced
- 1 cup tomato sauce
- 1 baguette, sliced
- 2 tbsp olive oil
- 1 clove garlic, minced

Instructions:

1. Layer zucchini, eggplant, and bell pepper in a baking dish with tomato sauce.
2. Bake at 375°F (190°C) for 30 minutes.
3. Brush baguette slices with olive oil and garlic, then toast.
4. Serve ratatouille with garlic bread.

Soba Noodles with Sesame-Ginger Dressing

Ingredients:

- 2 cups cooked soba noodles
- 1 tbsp sesame oil
- 1 tbsp soy sauce
- 1 tsp grated ginger
- ½ cup shredded carrots

Instructions:

1. Whisk sesame oil, soy sauce, and ginger.
2. Toss with soba noodles and carrots.

Roasted Cauliflower Steaks with Chimichurri

Ingredients:

- 1 head cauliflower, sliced into thick steaks
- 2 tbsp olive oil
- ½ cup parsley
- 1 clove garlic
- 1 tbsp red wine vinegar

Instructions:

1. Roast cauliflower at 400°F (200°C) for 25 minutes.
2. Blend parsley, garlic, vinegar, and olive oil for chimichurri.
3. Serve cauliflower with chimichurri on top.

Moroccan Spiced Carrot & Lentil Soup

Ingredients:

- 2 cups carrots, chopped
- 1 cup red lentils
- 1 onion, diced
- 2 cloves garlic, minced
- 1 tsp ground cumin
- 1 tsp ground coriander
- ½ tsp smoked paprika
- 4 cups vegetable broth
- 1 tbsp olive oil

Instructions:

1. Sauté onions and garlic in olive oil until softened.
2. Add carrots, lentils, and spices; stir well.
3. Pour in vegetable broth and simmer for 25 minutes.
4. Blend until smooth and serve warm.

Spinach & Ricotta Stuffed Peppers

Ingredients:

- 4 bell peppers, halved and seeds removed
- 1 cup ricotta cheese
- 1 cup fresh spinach, chopped
- ½ cup grated Parmesan cheese
- 1 tsp garlic powder
- Salt & pepper to taste

Instructions:

1. Preheat oven to 375°F (190°C).
2. Mix ricotta, spinach, Parmesan, garlic powder, salt, and pepper.
3. Stuff mixture into halved bell peppers.
4. Bake for 25 minutes until golden brown.

Vegan Sushi Rolls with Mango & Avocado

Ingredients:

- 1 cup sushi rice, cooked
- 1 tbsp rice vinegar
- 4 nori sheets
- 1 mango, sliced
- 1 avocado, sliced
- 1 cucumber, julienned

Instructions:

1. Mix cooked rice with rice vinegar.
2. Lay nori on a sushi mat, spread rice evenly.
3. Place mango, avocado, and cucumber on rice.
4. Roll tightly, slice, and serve.

Black Bean & Quinoa Stuffed Sweet Potatoes

Ingredients:

- 2 large sweet potatoes
- 1 cup cooked quinoa
- 1 can black beans, drained
- ½ cup corn kernels
- 1 tsp cumin
- 1 tsp chili powder
- ½ cup salsa

Instructions:

1. Roast sweet potatoes at 400°F (200°C) for 45 minutes.
2. Mix quinoa, black beans, corn, cumin, and chili powder.
3. Slice sweet potatoes open, stuff with quinoa mixture.
4. Top with salsa and serve.

Creamy Tomato Basil Soup with Grilled Cheese

Ingredients:

- 4 cups canned tomatoes
- 1 cup vegetable broth
- ½ cup heavy cream (or coconut milk for vegan)
- 1 small onion, diced
- 2 cloves garlic, minced
- ½ cup fresh basil leaves
- 2 tbsp olive oil

Instructions:

1. Sauté onion and garlic in olive oil.
2. Add tomatoes and broth, simmer for 20 minutes.
3. Blend until smooth, stir in cream and basil.
4. Serve with grilled cheese.

Thai Green Curry with Vegetables

Ingredients:

- 1 can coconut milk
- 2 tbsp Thai green curry paste
- 1 cup mixed vegetables (bell peppers, carrots, zucchini)
- 1 block tofu, cubed (optional)
- 1 tbsp soy sauce
- 1 tsp lime juice

Instructions:

1. Sauté green curry paste for 1 minute.
2. Add coconut milk, vegetables, and tofu.
3. Simmer for 10 minutes, stir in soy sauce and lime juice.
4. Serve with rice.

Spicy Kimchi Fried Rice

Ingredients:

- 2 cups cooked rice
- ½ cup kimchi, chopped
- 1 tbsp gochujang (Korean chili paste)
- 1 tbsp soy sauce
- 1 egg (optional)
- 1 green onion, sliced

Instructions:

1. Sauté kimchi in a pan for 2 minutes.
2. Add rice, gochujang, and soy sauce, stir-fry for 5 minutes.
3. Top with a fried egg and green onions.

Crispy Polenta with Roasted Mushrooms

Ingredients:

- 1 cup polenta
- 3 cups water
- ½ cup Parmesan cheese
- 1 tbsp olive oil
- 1 cup mushrooms, sliced

Instructions:

1. Cook polenta with water until thick, stir in Parmesan.
2. Spread in a dish and let cool, then slice.
3. Sauté mushrooms with olive oil.
4. Pan-fry polenta slices until crispy, serve with mushrooms.

Grilled Corn & Avocado Salad

Ingredients:

- 2 ears corn, grilled and kernels removed
- 1 avocado, diced
- ½ cup cherry tomatoes, halved
- ¼ cup red onion, diced
- 1 tbsp lime juice

Instructions:

1. Mix all ingredients in a bowl.
2. Toss with lime juice and serve.

Pumpkin & Sage Gnocchi

Ingredients:

- 1 cup mashed pumpkin
- 1½ cups flour
- ½ tsp salt
- 1 tbsp fresh sage, chopped
- 2 tbsp butter

Instructions:

1. Mix pumpkin, flour, and salt into a dough.
2. Roll into ropes, cut into small gnocchi pieces.
3. Boil until they float, then sauté in butter with sage.

Roasted Red Pepper Hummus with Pita Chips

Ingredients:

- 1 can chickpeas, drained
- 1 roasted red pepper
- 2 tbsp tahini
- 1 clove garlic
- 1 tbsp lemon juice
- 2 tbsp olive oil

Instructions:

1. Blend all ingredients until smooth.
2. Serve with pita chips.

Mango & Coconut Chia Pudding

Ingredients:

- 1 cup coconut milk
- 3 tbsp chia seeds
- 1 tbsp maple syrup
- ½ cup mango, diced

Instructions:

1. Mix coconut milk, chia seeds, and maple syrup.
2. Refrigerate overnight, top with mango before serving.

Vegan Tofu Scramble Breakfast Tacos

Ingredients:

- 1 block firm tofu, crumbled
- 1 tsp turmeric
- ½ tsp cumin
- ½ tsp smoked paprika
- ½ tsp garlic powder
- ½ cup diced bell peppers
- ½ cup diced onions
- 1 tbsp olive oil
- 4 small corn tortillas
- Avocado slices & salsa for topping

Instructions:

1. Heat olive oil in a pan and sauté onions and bell peppers until soft.
2. Add crumbled tofu and spices, stir well.
3. Cook for 5 minutes until flavors meld.
4. Serve in corn tortillas with avocado and salsa.

Balsamic Glazed Roasted Carrots

Ingredients:

- 1 lb carrots, peeled and cut lengthwise
- 2 tbsp balsamic vinegar
- 1 tbsp maple syrup
- 1 tbsp olive oil
- ½ tsp salt
- ½ tsp black pepper

Instructions:

1. Preheat oven to 400°F (200°C).
2. Toss carrots with balsamic vinegar, maple syrup, olive oil, salt, and pepper.
3. Spread on a baking sheet and roast for 25 minutes, flipping halfway.
4. Serve warm.

Indian Daal with Garlic Naan

Ingredients:

- 1 cup red lentils
- 1 onion, diced
- 2 cloves garlic, minced
- 1 tsp cumin
- 1 tsp turmeric
- ½ tsp garam masala
- 4 cups vegetable broth
- 1 tbsp olive oil

Instructions:

1. Heat oil and sauté onions and garlic until soft.
2. Add spices and stir for 30 seconds.
3. Add lentils and vegetable broth, simmer for 25 minutes.
4. Serve hot with garlic naan.

Stuffed Acorn Squash with Cranberries & Pecans

Ingredients:

- 2 acorn squash, halved and seeds removed
- 1 cup quinoa, cooked
- ½ cup dried cranberries
- ½ cup pecans, chopped
- 1 tsp cinnamon
- 1 tbsp maple syrup

Instructions:

1. Roast squash at 375°F (190°C) for 40 minutes.
2. Mix quinoa, cranberries, pecans, cinnamon, and maple syrup.
3. Fill squash halves with the mixture and bake for 10 more minutes.

Cabbage & Peanut Slaw with Lime Dressing

Ingredients:

- 2 cups shredded cabbage
- ½ cup shredded carrots
- ¼ cup chopped peanuts
- 2 tbsp lime juice
- 1 tbsp olive oil
- 1 tsp maple syrup

Instructions:

1. Whisk lime juice, olive oil, and maple syrup together.
2. Toss with cabbage, carrots, and peanuts.
3. Serve chilled.

Vegan Lasagna with Cashew Cheese

Ingredients:

- 12 lasagna noodles, cooked
- 2 cups marinara sauce
- 1 cup cashew cheese (blended cashews, lemon juice, nutritional yeast)
- 1 zucchini, sliced
- 1 cup spinach
- 1 cup mushrooms, chopped

Instructions:

1. Layer marinara sauce, noodles, cashew cheese, and vegetables in a baking dish.
2. Repeat layers and bake at 375°F (190°C) for 30 minutes.
3. Let cool before serving.

Mediterranean Stuffed Eggplant

Ingredients:

- 2 eggplants, halved and hollowed
- 1 cup cooked quinoa
- ½ cup diced tomatoes
- ¼ cup olives, chopped
- ½ tsp oregano
- 1 tbsp olive oil

Instructions:

1. Roast eggplants at 375°F (190°C) for 20 minutes.
2. Mix quinoa, tomatoes, olives, oregano, and olive oil.
3. Stuff eggplant halves and bake for 10 more minutes.

Roasted Garlic & Cauliflower Soup

Ingredients:

- 1 head cauliflower, chopped
- 1 head garlic, roasted
- 4 cups vegetable broth
- 1 cup coconut milk
- 1 tbsp olive oil

Instructions:

1. Roast cauliflower and garlic at 400°F (200°C) for 25 minutes.
2. Blend with vegetable broth and coconut milk until smooth.
3. Simmer for 10 minutes and serve warm.

Vegan Poke Bowl with Marinated Tofu

Ingredients:

- 1 block tofu, cubed
- 2 tbsp soy sauce
- 1 tsp sesame oil
- 1 cup cooked rice
- ½ cup diced cucumber
- ½ cup shredded carrots
- ½ avocado, sliced

Instructions:

1. Marinate tofu in soy sauce and sesame oil for 15 minutes.
2. Assemble bowl with rice, tofu, and vegetables.
3. Drizzle with extra soy sauce before serving.

Kale Caesar Salad with Crispy Chickpeas

Ingredients:

- 2 cups kale, chopped
- ½ cup chickpeas, roasted
- 2 tbsp vegan Caesar dressing
- 1 tbsp nutritional yeast

Instructions:

1. Toss kale with dressing and nutritional yeast.
2. Top with crispy roasted chickpeas.

Spiced Lentil & Sweet Potato Stew

Ingredients:

- 1 cup red lentils
- 1 sweet potato, diced
- 1 onion, diced
- 2 cloves garlic, minced
- 1 tsp cumin
- ½ tsp cinnamon
- 4 cups vegetable broth

Instructions:

1. Sauté onion and garlic in a pot.
2. Add lentils, sweet potatoes, spices, and broth.
3. Simmer for 30 minutes and serve warm.

Warm Farro Salad with Roasted Vegetables

Ingredients:

- 1 cup farro, cooked
- 1 zucchini, diced
- 1 red bell pepper, diced
- 1 cup cherry tomatoes, halved
- 1 small red onion, sliced
- 2 tbsp olive oil
- 1 tbsp balsamic vinegar
- ½ tsp salt
- ½ tsp black pepper
- ¼ cup chopped parsley

Instructions:

1. Preheat oven to 400°F (200°C).
2. Toss zucchini, bell pepper, tomatoes, and onion with olive oil, salt, and pepper.
3. Spread on a baking sheet and roast for 20-25 minutes.
4. Mix roasted vegetables with cooked farro, balsamic vinegar, and parsley.
5. Serve warm or at room temperature.

Black Bean & Corn Enchiladas

Ingredients:

- 1 can black beans, drained and rinsed
- 1 cup corn kernels
- 1 cup diced tomatoes
- 1 tsp cumin
- ½ tsp chili powder
- 8 small corn tortillas
- 1 cup enchilada sauce
- ½ cup chopped cilantro
- 1 tbsp olive oil

Instructions:

1. Preheat oven to 375°F (190°C).
2. Sauté black beans, corn, and tomatoes with olive oil and spices for 5 minutes.
3. Spoon mixture into tortillas, roll them up, and place in a baking dish.
4. Pour enchilada sauce over the top.
5. Bake for 20 minutes and garnish with cilantro before serving.

Jackfruit BBQ Sandwiches

Ingredients:

- 1 can young green jackfruit, drained and shredded
- 1 cup BBQ sauce
- ½ tsp smoked paprika
- ½ tsp garlic powder
- ½ tsp onion powder
- 1 tbsp olive oil
- 4 sandwich buns
- ½ cup coleslaw (optional)

Instructions:

1. Heat olive oil in a pan and sauté jackfruit with smoked paprika, garlic powder, and onion powder.
2. Add BBQ sauce and cook for 10 minutes, stirring occasionally.
3. Toast sandwich buns and fill them with BBQ jackfruit.
4. Top with coleslaw if desired and serve warm.

Japanese-Inspired Miso Glazed Tofu Bowl

Ingredients:

- 1 block firm tofu, cubed
- 2 tbsp miso paste
- 1 tbsp soy sauce
- 1 tbsp maple syrup
- 1 tbsp rice vinegar
- 1 tbsp sesame oil
- 1 cup cooked brown rice
- ½ cup shredded carrots
- ½ cup cucumber slices
- 1 tbsp sesame seeds

Instructions:

1. Preheat oven to 375°F (190°C).
2. Mix miso paste, soy sauce, maple syrup, rice vinegar, and sesame oil.
3. Toss tofu cubes in the glaze and bake for 20 minutes.
4. Serve tofu over brown rice with carrots and cucumbers.
5. Sprinkle with sesame seeds before serving.

Vegan Chocolate Avocado Mousse

Ingredients:

- 2 ripe avocados
- ¼ cup cocoa powder
- ¼ cup maple syrup
- 1 tsp vanilla extract
- ¼ cup almond milk
- Pinch of salt

Instructions:

1. Blend all ingredients in a food processor until smooth.
2. Adjust sweetness as needed.
3. Chill for 30 minutes before serving.
4. Top with fresh berries or shaved dark chocolate if desired.

www.ingramcontent.com/pod-product-compliance
Lightning Source LLC
LaVergne TN
LVHW081342060526
838201LV00055B/2802